COPING SKILLS
FOR CAREGIVERS

Nanette M. Holloway, MS, RN

Dedications

This book is dedicated to all the caregivers who give selflessly of time, energy, and love to loved ones in need. God bless you.

Table of Contents

Introduction

I was privileged to be a caregiver for my dad in his final year of life. He was 90, yet in my mind, never elderly. My age was forty.

He was diagnosed with cancer of the esophagus. I knew all the dreaded implications of the terminal disease. My occupation a registered nurse. More important I was his daughter.

My care was overshadowed by a kaleidoscope of undulating emotions of fear, powerlessness, dread, and endless worry about the obvious downward trajectory of my dad's health and his eventual final demise. The end of a well-lived yet stolen life.

Taken by the thief of cancer.

My mother died 23 years previous to lung cancer. I felt abandoned by each parent at their death. Orphaned at forty.

This book was born out of my own desperate needs during and after my caregiving journey. Self-neglect culminated in prolonged grief following my dad's death. My journey toward health included self-care strategies gleaned from grief counselors and Al-Anon principles. Al-Anon is a 12-Step program for family and friends of alcoholics.

This book is a companion to my memoir, _Before You Depart: God's Touch Before Eternity_. I was escorted through a chaotic year of caregiving by God's loving presence. My faith galvanized throughout the journey.

My hope and prayer are that my experience and the following compositions will assist you as you embark on your caregiving journey. Self-care is a necessary component as you sojourn the unknown.

My caregiving journey began with an audacious prayer for God's sustenance and help for the tumultuous days ahead.

God's Response

As you come to the garden of My Presence, bankrupted and empty, know that I understand. You have no strength for your journey. Know that I AM your strength. You have no joy for your journey. Know that I AM your joy. Lift up your hands in praise. For what is and what lies ahead. You do not know which task to pursue and which to lay down. I will make straight your path. Take one step at a time. I AM the lamp unto your feet and the light unto your path. I AM your refreshment and your portion. Let your cup be filled to overflowing. I AM the Living Water you desire to drink. Drink in refreshment and life. Let Me quench your thirst.

Cast all your cares on Me for I care for you. Do not be tempted to pick them up again. You are powerless to change them. I AM. I can take care of all of your needs and orchestrate what needs to be done in each instance. Come to the Garden of my presence. Rest in Me. Lay down your will and pray that My will be done on earth as it is in Heaven. Then believe. Love, The Father

Face of the Caregiver

Caregivers have many faces: Adult children taking care of aging parents, parents caring for sick children.

The face may be yours. Those faces include approximately 40 million individuals. One fourth are millennials.

Many caregivers work outside the home. Somehow they manage to carve out an estimated 21 hours of care for their loved ones in need.

The face of the caregiver may appear worn as the daily care demands all attention and energy. The tasks seem small and insignificant, albeit continuous.

Repeated questions and actions of the parent with Alzheimer's or the slow decline of chronic illness take a toll spiritually, mentally and emotionally.

Watching the steady decline of a loved one can be heart-wrenching. The once fiercely independent, self-sufficient individual now needs help with basic decision-making and bodily functions. The pending loss of a treasured relationship is ever present.

The caregiver, consumed by the needs of a loved one, often neglects her own needs. Self-neglect can lead to a health crisis for the caregiver. Such health concerns include but are not limited to depression, lowered immune response, frequent illness, and even death.

Regardless if you are new to the caregiver role or seasoned, apprehension and anxiety may include uninvited tormenting emotions. Signs of self-neglect include irritability, obsessing about your loved one, fatigue, impatience, sleeplessness, second guessing your decisions.

- Keep in mind that everyone is different and your symptoms of self-neglect may have a different twist. Be honest with yourself. Share your burden with a friend.

During my own caregiving experience my husband was a wonderful support person.

Other forms of support came through prayer from my church family, Hospice support services and the social worker from Hospice.

Self-Care Basics

Caregivers need to embrace self-care in order to prevent burnout.

- Have a quiet time in the morning. Prayer helps you start your monumental day of caregiving
- Set priorities
- Make a gratitude list. Purposely find ten things you are grateful for at the beginning or end of your day.
- Get plenty of sleep
- Eat healthy
- Exercise
- Learn to say "No"
- Set healthy boundaries
- Ask for help
- Take one day at a time
- Keep lines of communication open with your loved ones.
- Fight against false guilt. This situation is NOT your fault.

As a caregiver, I urge you to take special care of yourself. Your loved ones are depending on you. Your health, sanity and serenity are tantamount during this difficult season. Stay healthy so you can stay strong.

Scripture

"But they that wait for Jehovah shall renew their strength; they shall mount up with wings as eagles; they shall run, and not be weary; they shall walk, and not faint" (Isaiah 40:31 ASV).

Prayer

Father, I pray for all those who are in a caregiving role. I especially lift up those who may be new to the role. The demands can be emotionally, mentally, spiritually and physically exhausting. Give each one the strength, peace, joy, patience and long-suffering needed on a daily basis as they serve You and their loved one from heart and soul. Bless them as only You can. Amen.

Setting Priorities

Setting priorities as a caregiver can be difficult. New issues arise daily for the loved one in need of care. This can leave the caregiver bewildered and wondering what to do next.

Setting priorities was an afterthought in my journey of caregiving. First came the terminal diagnosis, followed by decisions of what treatments my dad should pursue, then more doctor visits added to an already busy routine.

But Dad's illness was the priority.

I vividly remember the night my dad needed to go to the emergency room. He was having trouble breathing. My two boys' friend was spending the night. At the time my husband worked nights.

Dad and I jumped in the car and made the forty-minute drive in thirty minutes. Before we left, the boys had strict instructions not to break anything. All I could do was pray that all would be well—at home and for my dad.

Sometimes priorities are made for us. Running to the ER was the priority.

Some priorities can be thought out. We are all busy. What can you do to carve out some serenity in your caregiving?

Start your day with prayer. My caregiving experience was steeped in prayer. God ushered me through the difficult experiences one day at a time.

Keep it Simple

- Limit what you can on your already full plate. What can you eliminate? House work may no longer be a priority. Clean what you can in ten minutes instead of the whole house. Clean a little bit every day.

- First things first.

- Limit your schedule: pare down to basics. Entertaining and socializing may need to be scaled back. Let your friends know what you are experiencing.

- Tending your loved one takes priority and may take extra time. Consider their pace which may be slower than the normal rushed pace. Plan ahead by adding extra time for errands and doctor appointments.

- Simplify meals: Add a salad night. Use your crockpot. Fix enough for leftovers.

- Ask for help. Maybe a friend can fix you dinner and deliver it to your house. Ask a friend to sit with your loved one when you run errands.

- Consolidate your errands and limit leaving the house.

- Get outside in the sunshine daily.

Keeping focus and limiting what's on the caregiving platter may help.

Scripture

"Pray, then, in this way: 'Our Father, who is in heaven, hallowed be Your name. Your kingdom come, Your will be done on earth as it is in heaven. 'give us this day our daily bread. And forgive us our debts, as we have forgiven our debtors [letting go of both the wrong and the resentment and do not lead us into temptation, but deliver us from evil. For Yours is the kingdom and the power and the glory forever. Amen" (Matthew 6:9-15 AMP).

Prayer

Father,

Bless each caregiver as she limits what is on her heaping plate. Help, her to let go of things that may not need to be done or can be put off. Help her to know Your will for the day, each day during this journey. Amen.

The Priority of Prayer

The priority of prayer is more than a nice idea—at least it was for me.

Facing the death of my ninety-year-old dad at age forty was a daunting reality, while I was homeschooling my two boys.

Most of my friends' grandparents were still living. Though they tried to understand, they were unable to relate to my situation. My husband was always willing to help and did his best to lighten the heavy load.

But God alone knew my needs. As I muddled through my caregiving season, God met me each morning. He provided hope, joy, strength and grace. At the end of my exhausting day,

I fell into bed. My dependence on God as my strength in the endless storm sustained me.

Daily I entered into God's all-consuming presence that felt like a euphoric wave of peace, joy and love. The wave washed over me and lingered. I lost connection with the world around me. All tension left my body, and my whole being relaxed. All worries were gone.

By the end of my devotion, my heart was filled with worship for God. His desire was for me to enter into His presence, come to Him, know Him, and require Him. I was refreshed and hopeful. Ready to face the day.

This is God's desire for you as well. He loves you and desires to care for you in your current circumstances. No matter how desperate or hopeless life appears, go to God in simple prayer. Tell Him all of your needs: large or small. He hears each cry.

Initially, when my dad was diagnosed with cancer of the esophagus, I prayed a brash prayer. My main concern was for the relationship between my dad and me. The once harmonious father-daughter relationship had become strained. He frequently belittled me, and I took quick offense. I prayed for God to re-establish what had been lost over the years.

Scriptures

"Casting all your cares [all your anxieties, all your worries, and all your concerns, once and for all] on Him, for He cares about you [with deepest affection, and watches over you very carefully]" (1 Peter 5:7 AMP).

"In my distress [when I seemed surrounded] I called upon the Lord and cried to my God for help; He heard my voice from His temple, and my cry for help came before Him, into His very ears" (Psalm 18:6 AMP).

Prayer

Almighty God, as caregivers we come to you with heavy hearts and fatigue. Fill us with Your all-consuming love, peace and joy in our caregiving journey. Give each caregiver the courage, strength and grace needed for each day. Help us to make prayer a priority. Amen.

Joy for the Caregiver

The joy of the Lord is our strength. As Christians we grow under stressful circumstances. Our faith in God stretches beyond current boundaries and expands. Our weak human frame and desperate need for help is revealed. Times of testing drive us to our knees in prayer to seek God's divine help.

During my caregiving season with my dad I was frustrated and overwhelmed. But God drew me into His loving presence with joy.

Certainly, I had read all the scriptures on joy and thought I understood them. But God wanted to reveal more. He desired for me to *experience* His joy on a deeper level.

First came the dreaded diagnosis that Dad had cancer of the esophagus. Big questions clouded my mind. How can I take care of Dad and my two boys at the same time? Am I ready for this? Fear rose in my heart. What was Dad's prognosis?

Then came the old familiar cloud of depression.

At that time the joy of the Lord as my strength and the fruit of the spirit were far from my mind. But God slowly worked His joy into my feeble, powerless spirit.

Thankfully, God's joy is greater than feelings of happiness that come and go with circumstances. Joy is a spiritual gift provided to the believer. Joy is not something worked up in the mind, but a gift — one of the fruits of the spirt:

"But the fruit of the Spirit is love, joy, peace, longsuffering, gentleness, goodness, faith, meekness, temperance: against such there is no law" (Galatians 5:22-23 KJV).

God manifested His joy to me during the long journey of caregiving in several ways. The following is an excerpt from my memoir, *Before You Depart: God's Touch before Eternity.*

God's Joy

During my quiet times with God, His presence met me in a new way. I had never been a morning person. Now I woke up early, as if God was urging me to enter into His presence through reading my Bible and having my prayer time.

God infused my devotions, thrilling my heart for an hour. Almost tangible waves of warmth and peace washed over me. All cares and worries ceased to matter. The Holy Spirit gave me a new joy, which is one of the gifts of the Spirit mentioned in Galatians 5:22 (NIV), *"But the fruit of the Holy Spirit, (The work*

22

which His Presence within accomplishes), is love, joy, peace, patience, kindness, faithfulness gentleness, self-control. Against such there is no law."

Nehemiah 8:10 reminded me, *"Do not grieve, for the joy of the Lord is your strength."*

Joy is a spiritual state of happiness and well-being, independent of surrounding circumstances. The joy God gave me was a deep happiness inside my heart and soul that no one could take.

This emotion was new for me. Most of my adult life I had struggled with depression. This joy was like a protection for my heart and emotions that overpowered the threat of depression. In the mornings I was filled with valiant purpose. God offered me His joy for the day ahead. I eagerly received His divine provision.

But by the end of the day I was exhausted. All strength and joy depleted. Home schooling the boys and caregiving for my dad consumed the long days.

In the evenings, the boys and I read aloud from *Rainbow Garden* by Patricia St John. The story was about a little girl who had to live with a family she did not know. The family introduced her to Christian values, scripture and prayer. The central theme of the story focused on the joy of the Lord. The scripture used was: *"You will show me the path of life; in Your presence is fullness of joy, at Your right hand are pleasures forevermore"* (Psalm 16:11 AMP).

Prayer for Today

Father, as caregivers approach their day, fill their hearts with unspeakable joy. The journey ahead appears daunting. Give each one strength, tenacity, and patience. Help them to cast each care upon you. Manifest your love and kindness to both the caregiver and the loved one. Let them know that you will never, never leave them or forsake them in their time of need. Amen.

An Attitude of Gratitude

The role of caregiver is fraught with responsibility, worry and often the feeling of *what's going to happen next?* Caring for a sick loved one can be chaotic and add to negative thinking.

Developing an attitude of gratitude may be a useful exercise for an overwhelmed caregiver.

Our attitude can affect not only our outlook on life, but also on the care given. The deliberate mental exercise of making a list of ten things we are grateful for produces a more positive outlook. Focusing on positives negates negative thoughts.

My own caregiving experience was emotional and stressful. Facing Dad's death while caring for him stretched my fragile emotions to the limit. At the age of forty, my coping skills were poor and underdeveloped. Homeschooling my two sons added to the stress.

During this time of my life a gratitude list was a foreign concept. Learning about this coping treasure did not occur until many years later during my journey of grief following Dad's death.

This coping tool would have been a wonderful benefit during the days of my dad's declining health. Continuing this mental exercise to this day has helped me to keep depression at bay.

Fostering an attitude of gratitude can be a challenge. Difficult seasons of life can drain us. Finding something—anything—to be grateful for seems impossible. Starting with the basics can help.

Gratitude List

1. The sun is shining

2. The birds are singing

3. A friend (be specific)

4. The loved one you are caring for

5. Any sleep the previous night

6. A roof over your head

7. Food in the pantry

8. _____

9. _____

10. _____

By the time your list is complete, your spirits may be lifted a little higher.

This daily exercise can also help train your mind to see all the goodness God has provided.

Sometimes we all need a reminder that life is good, and God is good…all the time.

Fill your thoughts with what is good:

Scripture

"Rejoice in the Lord always: again I will say, Rejoice. Let your forbearance be known unto all men. The Lord is at hand. In nothing be anxious; but in everything by prayer and supplication with thanksgiving let your requests be made known unto God. And the peace of God, which passeth all understanding, shall guard your hearts and your thoughts in Christ Jesus.

Finally, brethren, whatsoever things are true, whatsoever things are honorable, whatsoever things are just, whatsoever things are pure, whatsoever things are lovely, whatsoever things are of good report; if there be any virtue, and if there be any praise, think on these things. The things which ye both learned and received and heard and saw in me, these things do: and the God of peace shall be with you" (Philippians 4:4-9 ASV).

Prayer

Father, I thank you and praise You for all of the blessings You have given each one of us. Thank You for the loved ones we care for, and the provision of food, shelter, friends and family. We ask for energy and a good attitude during this difficult season. Please take special care of those in our care today and every day. Amen.

Helpful Resources

Gratitude Journal for Caregivers by Nanette M. Holloway, MS, RN available in color or black and white pictures. Available on Amazon: https://amzn.to/2Pv8Tlr

Psychologists are finding benefits from this simple daily exercise:

https://www.psychologytoday.com/us/basics/gratitude

Nutrition

Self-care for caregivers may be a foreign concept. Continual outpouring of physical, emotional and spiritual energy for a loved one can lead to caregiver burn out. Caregiving is continual with little reprieve.

Proper nutrition during your season of caregiving may be a challenge. High calorie, carbohydrate rich foods are convenient and taste best. Fast food is a constant temptation to those who are already tired.

Emotional eating may be a factor. Eating to comfort the spirit is a quick fix that can lead to more guilt and a larger waist line. Several people do the opposite and lose their appetites, not eating enough.

Let this be a gentle reminder in your caregiving journey. Give yourself time to fuel your body so you can think better and have the energy you need to care for your loved one.

- Have plenty of fruit available for a healthy snack or a quick breakfast.
- What's your favorite vegetable? Have some handy in the freezer for quick prep.
- Find your crock pot and put it to work. At the end of a tiring day, you'll have a nutritious dinner.
- Include a salad night. If you're too tired to prepare one there are plenty of alternatives.
    - Buy ready made at the grocery store
    - A fast-food alternative to a hamburger

Maybe you enjoy cooking. Give yourself permission for that activity. Have a friend help you with your loved one or keep you company while you cook.

Friends would love to help you. But they don't know what you need. Ask them to prepare a nutritious meal for you.

In conclusion, eat for health, not pleasure. Small changes add up. A little at a time, one day at a time.

The following recipe was a soup my mom made. My dad made a few changes. This recipe is full of vegetables and healthy ingredients ready to fuel you and your loved one. Cornbread is a hearty compliment.

Easy Beef Stew

2 Tablespoons of oil

Mrs. Dash to taste

Stew meat, beef

1 onion, chopped

1 small head of cabbage, cut in 1inch slices

1 turnip, peeled and cubed

2 carrots, peeled and sliced

1 46 oz. can of tomato juice, or V-8 juice

Directions: Brown stew meat in oil, add vegetables and canned juice, add Mrs. Dash. Cover and simmer until carrots are done.

Bon appetite.

Scripture

"Behold, that which I have seen to be good and to be comely is for one to eat and to drink, and to enjoy good in all his labor, wherein he laboreth under the sun, all the days of his life which God hath given him: for this is his portion" (Ecclesiastes 5:18 ASV).

Prayer

Father, bless our food to the nourishment of our bodies. During this time of added stress and focus on those who need us, help us to remember our need for fueling our bodies. Help us to consume food that will provide health and ready energy for each task ahead. As You supply us with spiritual sustenance, help us to limit eating for comfort or that emotional fix that is temporary and fleeting. Bless what we eat as well as our caregiving efforts. Amen.

Benefits of Exercise

Taking care of yourself as you care for a loved one may not yet be in the forefront of your mind. Constant worry and preoccupation with your loved one may consume all time and energy.

But what about you?

The benefits of exercise are well-documented. Physical movement makes our bodies feel better and can help clear our minds of caregiving stress.

During exercise, endorphins (good hormones) are released in the brain. Those feel-good hormones can keep depression at bay. You may experience an improved attitude and sleep better.

While a full-blown exercise program to improve your health may be too much for you at this time, simple changes can provide worthwhile rewards.

The exercise does not have to be strenuous and does not have to include the gym. Keep it simple.

- Walk down the street or around the block

- To increase your heart rate, walk briskly

- Try yoga

- Go to the library and check out an exercise CD

Just for a moment, let go of the responsibility and worry surrounding the caregiving role.

You may discover that you enjoy the exercise so much you increase the minutes to your walk.

Whatever you choose to do, start slowly.

Whatever your choice of exercise, be sure to stay hydrated.

Check with your doctor when starting any new exercise program.

My daily exercise program began as a student at Oral Roberts University. We were required to get daily aerobic points. By the time I graduated, daily exercise was part of my lifestyle, a definite health benefit.

When my mother was diagnosed with lung cancer, I was training for a ten-k run. Knowing the benefits of jogging, I continued my efforts beyond her death and completed the Tulsa Run. The activity relieved stress and helped limit some of the depression related to grief.

When taking care of my dad, walking was beneficial.

Now that I'm older my choices of exercise include swimming, walking and cycling.

Small efforts toward self-care can add up. Get refreshed through an activity of your choice.

Scripture

"Therefore, seeing we also are compassed about by so great a cloud of witnesses, let us lay aside every weight, and the sin which doth so easily beset us, and let us run with patience the race that is set before us" (Hebrews 12:1 KJV).

Prayer

Father, help caregivers in the journey that lies ahead. Help them to seek and find avenues of exercise that will benefit the body, mind and spirit. Help them. Strengthen them as they run the race you have set before them. Be glorified in the loving care they provide on a daily basis. Amen.

Helpful Resources

https://www.mayoclinic.org/healthy-lifestyle/stress-management/in-depth/exercise-and-stress/art-20044469

Get Outside

A breath of fresh air and stopping to smell the roses hold a wealth of merit. Especially for the caregiver occupied by endless tasks.

Make getting outside your daily goal.

A breath of fresh air does the body and mind good. As we step outside, we change our focus to the surrounding environment. Suddenly the air quality is improved. Environmentalists claim the outdoor air is up to five times cleaner than indoor stale air. So, breathe in the freshness of the great outdoors.

Fresh air provides plant and organic substances that boost the immune system. These substances known as phytoncides protect plants from harmful bacteria and insects. They hold benefits for us too. Be sure to get your daily dose.

In Japan the practice of forest therapy is called Shinrin Yoku. Research shows this practice lowers blood pressure, slows the heart rate, lessens depression and hostility.

Time in nature quiets the mind and promotes creativity — essentials for a stressed caregiver.

An outing should include deliberate focus on the breeze, the air temperature, perhaps the birds singing, or the color of the leaves or grass.

The great outdoors beckon. We see the fall foliage or feel that brisk winter air which provides a mental slowdown for greater clarity and a clearing of the mind.

The benefits of sunlight cannot be overlooked. Our bodies depend on sunlight for Vitamin D production. Vitamin D deficiencies can lead to increased blood pressure, diabetes, infections, poor immunity, and contribute to colon cancer, prostate cancer, breast cancer and multiple sclerosis. Symptoms of vitamin D deficiency include muscle weakness, pain, fatigue, depression, mood changes and bone loss.

Sunlight also increases serotonin levels, thereby increasing energy, a calm mood, positivity, and focus. Sunlight energizes the T-cells that fight infections.

Ample natural sunlight promotes sleep. As we age, our eyes lose their ability to absorb light, contributing to insomnia.

A fifteen to twenty-minute stroll in the sunshine three times weekly will provide the body's need for vitamin D production.

Perhaps you might spend some time on the porch drinking coffee or tea. Lift a pantleg or a sleeve to optimize exposure to the sun. Include your loved one. They need vitamin D as well.

Getting outside can provide a means of temporary escape from the responsibilities of caregiving.

Going for a walk was on my daily agenda while caring for my dad. A short break in the outdoor expanse provided a brief respite from the encroaching sadness, illness and the pungent odors of various treatments.

Dad defied the image of the model patient. Often my patience was stretched beyond a comfortable tolerance. Since Dad was hard-of-hearing, communication was difficult. An outdoor break was always welcome.

Scripture

"For You formed my innermost parts; You knit me [together] in my mother's womb. I will give thanks and praise to You, for I am fearfully and wonderfully made; Wonderful are Your works, and my soul knows it very well. My frame was not hidden from You, when I was being formed in secret, and intricately and skillfully formed [as if embroidered with many colors] in the depths of the earth" (Psalms 139:13-15 AMP).

Prayer

Father, you have provided us with warm sunshine to brighten our days. The provision of vitamin D through sunlight on our skin is another keen example of how our bodies are wonderfully made. Help each caregiver and their loved one to get outside daily and enjoy your wonderful creation. Amen.

The Priority of Sleep

The priority of sleep may be difficult to attain. Caregiving is chaotic at times. The caregiver may be frazzled and fatigued.

The body is tired, the mind weary, yet unable to shut down from worries or what if's that may occur during some desperately needed shut eye.

Needs of the loved ones we care for are varied. Thankfully my dad was a good sleeper. He went to bed early and got up early. I adjusted my schedule to his. Early to bed, earlier to rise.

I squeezed in my quiet time with the Lord and managed some family time with my children. By that time, my dad was ready for his day.

Not only was he a good sleeper, but he had his own living quarters close to my house. This made my sleep easier.

Shutting down my mind was more difficult. I checked on him before his bed time, then compulsively made sure his light was out. That meant all was fine. Then a quick check in the morning to see if his light was on. Another good sign.

Suggestions to Promote Sweet Slumber

- Bypass the nap unless your situation dictates one. If needed, opt for a twenty-minute power nap.

- Limit caffeinated beverages. Coffee in the morning. Taper off by noon.

- Dodge those late-night meals and snacks. Calories provide energy not needed while we sleep.

- Steer clear of screen light before bed. Yes, this includes phones, computers and tablets.

- Clear your mind of anything that may be pending for your loved one. Let go and let God. Leave the situation in the capable hands of God for the night.

Fatigue leads to impatience, grumpiness and a poor attitude. Your loved one deserves your best.

The hope and the goal is a good night's sleep. Then you can rise refreshed and ready to start a new day of caregiving.

Scripture

"When you lie down, you will not be afraid; when you lie down, your sleep will be sweet" (Proverbs 3:24 NASB).

Prayer

Father,

I pray for the weary caregivers in need of sleep. Let them fall into a deep slumber and awaken refreshed. Multiply their sleep. Help them to cast all of their cares onto you, trusting each detail of their loved one to you. You are faithful. We praise You and thank You in advance for a good night's sleep. Amen.

Helpful Resources

AmericanSleepAssociation
https://www.sleepassociation.org/about-sleep/sleep-hygiene-tips/

The Power of Creativity

Being creative is a great diversion from the mundane routine.

Creativity is the ability to design new and exciting ways of doing things. Coming up with new ideas, alternatives to the status quo, problem-solving and fun ways to entertain ourselves.

Dictionary.com defines creativity as "the ability to transcend traditional ideas, rules, patterns, relationships, or the like, and to create meaningful new ideas, forms, methods, interpretations, etc., originality, progressiveness, or imagination."

Use your current knowledge in a new and different way.

In other words, change things up. Step out of your comfort zone. Dig deep. Restart a hobby long forgotten.

Use some imagination in your everyday routine. What can you do differently while caring for your loved one?

A lighthearted activity for both you and your loved one would benefit you both.

We use creativity on a daily basis. The creative process provides us with satisfaction and an increase in self-esteem.

Creativity for the caregiver provides desperately needed diversions from problems close at hand that will not go away any time soon. Self-care tactics are tantamount to provide a moment of sanity in an environment of confusion, illness and fatigue.

Hand work, such as knitting or crocheting can be mindless, yet fulfilling.

My creative outlet was making soap. The craft kept my mind off the problems at hand and provided me with much needed diversion.

Dad declined to the point that leaving the house became difficult. I needed time at home to learn the delightful chemical reaction process of saponification. I quickly learned that the entire process required about two hours of undivided attention. Any slip-ups and my batch could be ruined.

The mysterious chemical reaction eventually reached the point of pouring into a container. I wrapped the containers with blankets to keep the unfinished soap in a warm, dark place. Then came the two-weeks wait for the final curing process.

Anticipation of the finished product was close to unbearable. Finally, the once warm, creamy liquid had magically turned into soap, ready to be used for bathing and handwashing.

I enjoyed making soap so much I established a soap company called Oklahoma Rose Pure and Natural Soaps. Although a fun season, my soap company is no longer in business.

How can you use the power of imagination to enhance your life during this season of caregiving?

Scripture

"For we are His workmanship [His own master work, a work of art], created in Christ Jesus [reborn from above—spiritually transformed, renewed, ready to be used] for good works, which God prepared [for us] beforehand [taking paths which He set], so that we would walk in them [living the good life which He prearranged and made ready for us] " (Ephesians 2:10 AMP).

Prayer

Father,

We come before you today. Help us to use our imagination to make the ordinary extraordinary and add wonder and satisfaction to our daily lives in simple ways. Amen.

Caregiver Emotions

My emotions as a caregiver were intense and all-consuming. The stress surrounding the role of caregiving often distorted and amplified emotions. Unhealthy family dynamics raised their ugly heads, demanding attention at the most awkward of times.

Guilt was often a central emotion triggered by the demands and anger of my dad who did not feel good. Guilt feelings were compounded by my people-pleasing efforts, which never worked. An unhealthy dose of perfectionism topped off the emotional heap.

Trying to fix everything failed, which left me frustrated and guilt-ridden. Feelings of powerlessness rose up. Unchecked guilt led to shame and poor self-esteem.

When Dad displayed unprovoked anger, the perfectionist in me suffered. Guilt occurred when my own shortcomings surfaced in response to difficult situations.

Maybe my tone was too harsh or my attitude bad due to lack of sleep and stress. My performance was frequently short of unrealistic expectations. More guilt.

Guarding against false guilt can benefit your caregiving journey. You did not cause the illness or chronic condition your loved one is experiencing.

- Let go of what you cannot control: illness, anger, poor appetite, poor attitudes, arguing, and the progression of disease. This can be an endless list.

- Accept what you cannot control. Yes, this is difficult.

- Everyone is doing the best job possible, and may be struggling.
  Let go of perfection. Caregiving is messy.

- Allow yourself to make mistakes and be human.

- Let go of unrealistic expectations.

Remember you are doing a difficult if not impossible job. All you can do is your best, one day at time. Remind yourself you are doing a wonderful job taking care of your loved one.

Keep going.

Scripture

"For it is by grace [God's remarkable compassion and favor drawing you to Christ] that you have been saved [actually delivered from judgment and given eternal life] through faith. And this [salvation] is not of yourselves [not through your own effort], but it is the [undeserved, gracious] gift of

God; not as a result of [your] works [nor your attempts to keep the Law], so that no one will [be able to] boast or take credit in any way [for his salvation]" (Ephesians 2:8-9 AMP).

Prayer

Father,

I lift up all those whose hearts are burdened by guilt. False guilt. The guilt that grips our emotions, plummets our self-esteem and defines us through shame. Let caregivers realize they are not responsible for anger, illness, and unmet needs beyond their scope of care. Give the assurance that Your grace is sufficient in all things. Help them to loosen the grip on what they cannot control and release the burden of guilt into Your mighty hands. Amen.

Frustration and Forgiveness

Frustration and unforgiveness are like small pebbles wedged in the bottom of a shoe. If the pebble is neglected, a festering blister develops. Further neglect leads to the crippling wound of bitterness.

Caregiving can be steeped with irritation. New needs rise on a continual basis. Daily changes and lost abilities equal greater dependence on the caregiver.

Perhaps your loved one has a demanding personality, or dementia with childlike behavior asking the same question several times an hour. Maybe your efforts are unappreciated. Or a new caregiver attempts to step in and assist only to be met with resistance and resentment.

Whatever your situation, frustrations arise. Dealing with small irritations at the onset can prevent anger that builds into bitter resentment.

Some frustration may be alleviated by the acceptance of what is. We cannot change the aging process and what it has chosen to steal from a loved one. Nor the disease process that consumes their body. Medications may slow the process, and make them more comfortable, but they may not fix the inevitable decline.

While taking care of my dad I held on to denial, refusing to accept that my dad could be anything but stubbornly strong and independent. In reality, he became stubborn and needy under the diagnosis of cancer of the esophagus. His once strong muscular frame morphed into an emaciated skeleton covered by skin.

My denial created unrealistic expectations my father could never meet. His needs remained.

Frustration and anger are miserable burdens to bear. The negative emotions color all of life, fill hearts and consume the spirit.

Hence, bitterness and resentment take over.

Forgiveness

Frequent forgiveness and prayer may help. God alone knows the situation, and the difficulties in your day. Forgiving can keep our hearts tender. God helps us with that difficult spiritual task. We require divine help from our loving Father.

Detachment

Detachment is another remedy. A strategy to distance oneself from a problem by not reacting or refusing to participate. For example, it always takes two people to argue. But what if you choose not to argue? The other person may attempt several times to engage your participation. Each time you detach, you resist to engage in a fueled exchange. Eventually the other person will give up.

A classic example for a caregiver may be the temptation to argue with an individual who has experienced memory loss. The effort is futile. Your loved one is unable to respond with logic or reasoning. Yet the argument continues through countless repetitions of the same issue. Perhaps your loved one is unable to remember details and answers previously discussed. The person once able to carry on an engaging conversation or remember details for the next doctor visit has helplessly declined beyond simple understanding.

The only person bothered by the pointless interaction is you, the frustrated caregiver.

The conversation is narrowed. The attention span of your loved one is limited. The outlook on life is diminished to now, the simple near future, or possibly the past.

Much like that of a two-year-old, simplicity has taken over and self is on the throne. The two-year-old mentality comparison is not meant to offend but rather to assist in slowing the pace and a gentle reminder that reality has changed for your aging loved one. Join them in their reality and their new existence.

Let the conversation and your frustration drop. Gently remind yourself that their mind is unable to track like yours and mine.

During my caregiving journey, Dad was often angry. He seemed to take all his anger out on me. My sensitive nature could not wrap my mind around his irritability.

Looking back through more mature eyes, I now see Dad in his last days, attempting to make it through another day of chronic arthritic pain. Maybe his irritation was because of relentless pain, unable to find a comfortable position for his age-worn joints. Perhaps he was just angry that his time was short. Or maybe he found me the safe target for outbursts, knowing I would still love him — no matter what.

Detach from the problem, not the person. Perhaps a soft answer to deescalate a problem that has little merit. An Al-Anon slogan that might help is "how important is it?"

Letting things drop may improve sanity for yourself as well as your loved one.

When tensions rise, try the diversion technique. Find some common ground and discuss something positive. Change the subject. You can also distance yourself and go outside.

Another Al-Anon coping tip is "letting go of being right or having the last word." Insisting on the last say creates tension and strife. Again, "how important is it?"

Scripture

"But have nothing to do with foolish and ignorant speculations [useless disputes over unedifying, stupid controversies], since you know that they produce strife and give birth to quarrels" (2 Timothy 2:23 AMP).

"And forgive us our debts, as we forgive our debtors" (Matthew 6:12 KJ21).

Prayer

Father,

I lift up each caregiver approaching daily caregiving. Provide peace and harmony in their households. Help each caregiver who is experiencing tensions in relationships. Let them find the strategies needed to deal with disagreements and frustration. Keep their hearts free from bitterness. Assist them in changes they may need to make. Help them find the daily routines that will accommodate their loved one. Amen.

Resources

Forgive and Forget: Healing the Hurts we Don't Deserve by Lewis B. Smedes Available on Amazon: https://amzn.to/37eqEht

Lewis B. Smeads has several books and workbooks available concerning forgiveness.

Isolation for the Caregiver

Isolation is a condition that creeps up out of nowhere. We are suddenly engulfed in loneliness, despair and seclusion.

As the primary caregiver for my dad, isolation encroached slowly.

Initially my routine included a monthly homeschool Mom's night-out meeting and frequent outings with my boys. Church provided a means to connect with other believers on a weekly basis. But as Dad's condition grew worse, I opted to stay close to home.

Any outings were short. To the grocery store in a rush, only if my husband was home. I feared Dad might fall in my absence.

Or something worse like a medical emergency and no one home. My dad seemed to weaken by the day.

The last time we had dinner with friends, my mind was overtaken by preoccupied uneasiness. What might Dad need in my absence? The host was wonderful and accepted my apology as we quickly ate and ran home. My obsession taught me to stay home and close by while my dad remained on this earth.

Friends slowly disappeared, unable to relate to my caregiving situation and the emotions surrounding the mounting daily responsibilities. Unaware of the seriousness of isolation, the condition broadened and engulfed me. Alone and wrestling with the pending death of my dad.

Hospice was a benefit. The social worker seemingly hand-picked by God. She listened to my concerns and sojourned my difficult path. She supported me when faced with difficult decisions and affirmed my feelings without judgement.

Social isolation can be detrimental to our health. The condition left unchecked leads to loneliness, culminating in adverse effects, emotionally and mentally. Long periods of isolation leave us depressed, increase mental stress, contribute to insomnia and emotional exhaustion — even physical manifestations such as cardiac disease and diabetes. Chronic isolation has increased the risk of higher mortality rates and suicide.

Depression and isolation are often interconnected. One condition can lead to the other in a vicious cycle.

Suicide can be a factor as well.

Cognitive function becomes dulled. Individuals exhibit increased forgetfulness and possible confusion. Studies conclude dementia is increased with chronic isolation.

Those who face the pain of social isolation often turn to substance abuse in an attempt to self-medicate. One problem burgeons into the trap of addiction.

God created us as social beings. We need others in our lives. Social interaction stimulates the mind and stirs emotions of joy and connectedness. Being around others gives meaning to life. Positive social interaction provides us with love, acceptance and a positive self-esteem. Belonging is a primary need that must be fostered for optimal mental health.

Take precautions to avoid the loneliness of isolation. Small interactions during the day are beneficial. Talk to a trusted loved one on the phone for fifteen minutes daily. Use social media to connect briefly with those who live far away. Stay connected to others and the outside world.

Scripture

"Behold, how good and how pleasant it is for brethren to dwell together in unity" (Psalm 133:1 AMPC).

Prayer

Father, I lift up each caregiver and their loved ones who may be suffering from isolation. Help us to avoid this tendency in the midst of stress, illness, loss and continual change. Help us to reach out, beyond our comfort zone if needed, to those we love and in turn love us. Help us to renew our minds daily in your wonderful word. Amen.

Helpful Resources

Hospice Questions: https://www.webmd.com/palliative-care/hospice-care#

Home Health Questions: https://www.medicare.gov/what-medicare-covers/whats-home-health-care

For Hospice or home health companies:

Google Hospice near me

Google Home Health near me

Consider counseling for depression or substance abuse. Some counselors even come to the home or may provide a video chat. Look for a counselor that specializes in caregivers and end-of-life issues.

Family Communication

Accurate and healthy communication is difficult. Especially when caregiving issues for a loved one arise.

As you approach your caregiving journey, keep the lines of communication open with family. Or at least try. One more challenge on the caregiving platter.

Hopefully you are blessed with siblings and extended family who enjoy healthy communication. And they are able to speak openly about the difficult subjects of caregiving and end of life issues.

Family dynamics often take a downward spiral during a crisis. Weddings, funerals, graduations, births and other intense life events stir the pot of unresolved family conflict.

My own experience in the communication arena was not textbook perfect. Conflict, tears and anger rose frequently on all sides.

The best part of my story is that everything ended up on a good note for everyone. Each of us experienced unsolicited growth during the difficult caregiving process.

Chances are your family dynamics may not be optimal. Knowing that conflict will be part of the process may help. That knowledge equals success.

Set Healthy Goals

- Always try for a civil conversation.

- Keep your tone even and calm. This practice may help set the mood for a peaceful interaction.

- Prepare a list of suggestions for a plan of care:

  o Home health may be a benefit. Home health agencies offer support services for those with chronic illnesses. Depending on the need, a licensed nurse will offer weekly visits providing care and education for your loved one.

  o If your loved one has a terminal diagnosis, Hospice may be beneficial. The Hospice team includes a registered nurse, Hospice aide, social worker, and chaplain. All disciplines work together to provide care to patient and family as they face end-of-life issues.

- Keep an open mind to others' feelings and suggestions that may differ from yours.

- Listen respectfully to opposing views. Someone else may have a good solution.

- Siblings don't always agree. That's okay.

- Keep in mind that all concerned may be frightened and react out of fear.

  o Anger is often a mask for fear.

  o Fear of the future, the unknown and the possible pending death concerning a loved one may be a factor.

  o Anxiety over interacting and facing difficult decisions.

- If you are the primary caregiver, gently assert your concerns and ideas.

- Include your loved one as you plan his future.

- People may experience growth throughout the crisis. Be patient with yourself and others.

- Pray before major decisions or interactions occur.

Scripture

"Do not let unwholesome [foul, profane, worthless, vulgar] words ever come out of your mouth, but only such speech as is good for building up others, according to the need and the occasion, so that it will be a blessing to those who hear [you speak]" (Ephesians 4:29 AMP).

Prayer

Father, I lift up each family involved in the care of a loved one. Bring strength and comfort to each family as they face health care or end-of-life issues. Let the communication in each family be clear and void of strife. Let there be peace in each family interaction. Where there is strife between family members, bring peace. Where there is hurt, bring healing. Where there is disagreement, bring harmony. May all concerned let go of their will and let your will be done. Amen.

Resources for Home Health or Hospice

https://www.medicare.gov/what-medicare-covers/whats-home-health-care

https://www.webmd.com/healthy-aging/hospice-care#1

Establishing Healthy Boundaries

Establishing healthy boundaries for the caregiver is difficult. Good boundaries are essential for any healthy relationship.

But as a caregiver, establishing boundaries is compounded by role reversal. Simply stated, this reversal consists of the child parenting the parent in need of care.

Reversing roles is like stepping into a muddy swamp.

My dad was fiercely independent, accustomed to being in control, and just plain stubborn. He did not take kindly to new boundaries.

Multiple tense moments followed my first attempts. But with time, Dad became more responsive.

Healthy boundaries create peace in relationships. When setting boundaries, be clear about what you want and need.

Since one of my needs was to homeschool my children in the mornings, I needed Dad to make doctor appointments in the afternoons. He wanted morning appointments. I had to clearly and calmly (that's the hard part) tell him what I needed.

Learn to say "No." Telling my dad "No" was hard, because I was used to catering to all of his needs. As his needs increased, the need to set limits increased.

Setting boundaries was important to protect what little time I had. Getting up early provided me time to myself and a quiet time. That was followed by homeschool with my children. Then for a break I fixed breakfast for Dad and we had coffee together. The boys watched cartoons. More homeschool. After school I checked on my dad again.

Another way I was able to take care of myself was making soap. The process took about two hours. The craft was therapeutic and provided distraction. Vegetable gardening was also at the top of my creative list. On good days Dad helped and enjoyed a daily garden tour.

My husband was off on Saturdays, so we enjoyed family time on that day. We took Dad out to eat for lunch for as long as he was able. One day my husband had to carry Dad into the restaurant, but we all enjoyed a catfish dinner.

Good boundaries begin with "No." A small word, yet difficult to say. "No" is the other magic word, essentially paired with "please" and "thank you."

Caregivers and individuals in caring occupations typically give beyond their comfort zones. Others may take advantage of their giving nature.

The lack of boundaries leads to becoming a door mat or a target for manipulation.

Being a people-pleaser compounds the situation. Trying to make everyone happy can end in a futile waste of energy and resources.

Finding balance is the key. Most of us have grown up doing what we've been told. Saying "No" to those in authority stirs discomfort and creates guilt.

A caregiver responsible for an aging parent requires an occasional "No."

My own experience in telling my father "No" was difficult. One snowy day he had a doctor appointment. My husband was on the road in a diesel truck and advised us against getting out in the weather.

Telling my dad we had better not go, resulted in him getting mad and making the 30-mile trip himself.

Still mad when he got home, he wondered why I wouldn't take him to the appointment.

I replied, "What am I going to do if I get stranded with a ninety-year-old man?" End of conversation.

Saying "No" makes us uncomfortable. What if the other person gets mad? Or what if this boundary results in the loss of a friend?

When people love you they will get over being mad. If you lose a friend over a boundary issue, she may not have been a good friend after all.

Feelings of anger or resentment toward your loved one is a good clue that you need to say "No." Often feelings of anger build when we stuff our feelings. When we do something we are not comfortable with, or do something we do not want to do, we become angry. That anger eventually turns into resentment.

Learning to Set Boundaries is a Journey

Thankfully my own journey landed me in a twelve-step program: AL-Anon Family Support Group. The structure of the meetings and loving help from members provided tools needed to make good boundaries and learn to say "No."

Setting boundaries takes practice and good communication skills. The end result is a happier you. Healthy boundaries are like a secret weapon of safety we give to ourselves. Establishing them takes time and practice.

The creation of healthy boundaries will eventually create a safe space for you. Setting limits around unhealthy behavior is initially difficult.

Take care of yourself with healthy boundaries. Begin your journey today.

Scripture

"But let your statement be, 'Yes, yes' or 'No, no' [a firm yes or no]…" (Matthew 5:37 AMP).

Prayer

Father, setting boundaries with those we love is difficult. Help each caregiver to learn the benefit of boundaries. Help them find the support they need to begin to set healthy boundaries for improved relationships with family as well as friends. Give them peace and reassurance as they begin the difficult work of saying "No". Bless each effort they make in this foreign journey. Amen.

Helpful Resources

The Language of Letting Go by Melody Beattie, available on amazon: https://amzn.to/2J38k2D

Boundaries: When to Say Yes, How to Say No to Take Control of Your Life by Dr. Henry Cloud and Dr. John Townsend available on amazon: https://amzn.to/2V5vkjM

http://boundaries.me
by Dr. Henry Cloud

Al-Anon Family Groups https://al-anon.org/

Alzheimer's Disease

Alzheimer's Disease is commonly described as the long good-bye. Individuals with Alzheimer's may live as long as seven to twenty years following the diagnosis. Progression of the disease varies.

As Baby Boomers continue to age it is estimated that one out of ten persons 65 years and over will have the devastating disease. Caregivers bear the brunt of a heavy burden, day in and day out.

Generally, the disease is divided into four stages, although symptoms may overlap.

Early Stage

Mild, short term memory loss and forgetfulness occur. Inability to find the correct word is common. Repeating the same thing over and over and the inability to remember the answers to questions just answered minutes previous. Changes in judgement may occur. Decline may be slow.

Mild Stage

Individuals may need some direction in order to carry out the activities of daily living. A change in personality and flat emotional responses may be noticed.

Moderate Stage

The disease progression is characterized by the inability to choose the correct clothing for the season or match colors. The ability to cook or remember their own address may be lost. Simple activities such as looking at photos or listening to music are beneficial.

Final Stage

Full-time care may be required. Assistance with all activities of daily living becomes necessary. Help with bathing, toileting, eating become the norm. Vocabulary is limited to a few words. Individuals may need help eating or have food placed in front of them. The process of eating becomes prolonged. Food may eventually need to be put in the blender for ease of swallowing.

Sundowning Syndrome

Some individuals experience Sundowning Syndrome, although many do not. Symptoms include increased agitation, confusion, or anxiety in the late afternoon or evening hours. Some individuals hallucinate or pace.

The cause of Sundowners is unknown. Diminished light seems to trigger symptoms.

Provide adequate light to limit shadows. Keep a strict routine. Any change in routine can trigger agitation or confusion. Even changing caregivers for a respite may increase symptoms. People with Alzheimer's become dependent on their caregivers.

Keep it simple

Approach daily life in simple slow motion. Cognition is slow, so hurry may upset or confuse your loved one. The daily life focus is in the now. This moment. Lower your expectations.

Try to keep your loved one as independent as possible for as long as possible. For instance, with grooming you may have to show them the toothbrush, then give step-by-step instructions on tooth brushing. Avoid giving lengthy instructions or too many steps at a time. Too much information adds to confusion.

Allow them to dress themselves if possible. The ability to choose matching outfits may be beyond their capability. Lay their clothes out or give them one item at a time to put on.

Simplify meals. Limit food choices. Try one or two items on a plate. Small frequent meals may be a good strategy. If weight loss occurs try protein drinks such as Ensure or Boost.

Assisting your loved one with bathing may become necessary. One individual I took care of while a Hospice nurse refused to bathe. The family was unable to figure out why. Turns out he was afraid of falling. A shower chair, a hand-held shower head and grab bars helped him feel secure. With time he trusted the nurse's aide to help with his shower.

The noise of the television and television content may increase confusion. They may have trouble distinguishing reality from fantasy. They may think what is happening on the news is happening to them.

Involve your loved one in simple chores. Folding laundry, sweeping or dusting may occupy their mind for a short time and improve self-esteem. Keep expectations of perfection out of the picture.

Engage your loved one by singing popular songs from their generation. One individual loved to sing "You are my Sunshine." She was otherwise nonverbal.

Not everyone is mentally equipped to deal with the devastating decline seen with Alzheimer's disease. Caregivers may opt for the outside help of a memory unit or nursing home. These decisions are individual to each person and circumstance. One deterring factor to nursing homes is price. Not all individuals can afford the cost of long-term care.

Some individuals shun the idea of long-term care. If you fall into this category elicit the help of Home Health or Hospice.

Placement of your loved one into a facility under any circumstance is a difficult, heart-wrenching decision. When I conceded to this decision for my dad, my emotions were flooded with grief, despair, uncertainty and guilt. The difficult decision left me emotionally destitute. On the other hand, I knew that I could no longer take care of him.

Scripture

"Even to your old age I am He, and even to your advanced old age I will carry you! I have made you, and I will carry you; Be assured I will carry you and I will save you." (Isaiah 46:4 AMP).

Prayer

Father,

Bless each caregiver and their loved ones who are facing the challenges of Alzheimer's Disease or dementia. Provide patience, and longsuffering during this marathon of care. Comfort the heart of grief and provide joy in the moments that pass. Help us to see life through your eyes: divine, sacred, a gift from you. Always. Amen.

Helpful Resources

Alzheimer's Association: https://www.alz.org/help-support

Google Home Health near me.

Google Hospice near me.

Sometimes they Forget by RJ Thesman, available on Amazon: http://amzn.to/2uqi3mT

Role Reversal

Role reversal often results in fiery reactions as the adult child parents the parent. The reversal becomes necessary when aging parents become a danger to themselves or require more help.

A classic example of this dynamic is taking the car keys away. Driving equals independence, an activity not easily relinquished.

One aging parent drove her car into a pond. The family could no longer put off the decision. The car was totaled. Although unharmed, the mildly confused woman was unable to comprehend why she could no longer drive. The car was not replaced. Her new reality, homebound and dependent, slowly morphed into acceptance.

My own experience was easier. Dad left the car running over night. This occurred twice. Eventually, he was too weak to travel independently. Thankfully a confrontation was avoided. My dad relinquished his keys.

However the tables turn long before taking the car keys. Responsibilities once handled with ease by your loved one now necessitate help. For example, my dad was hard of hearing and was unable to order his medications on the pharmacy telephone prompt. A new responsibility for me. I became the parent and gradually took over his medical needs.

Role reversal creates discomfort. New roles require learning on both sides.

I was used to taking orders from my dad and being the good daughter. We both had to learn how to let me be the responsible parent while he became the good son.

Awareness

Awareness of the need for role reversal is the first step in transitioning. Be respectful of your parents' wishes and preferences. Allow them to keep as much independence and choice as long as possible.

Remember your loved one does not like the aging process and loss of independence any more than you do. They may be grieving this loss.

When my dad downsized, he parted with several possessions and created a storage area for other items. Not realizing his feelings, I began to clean out the storage area of what I thought was junk. This angered him. Allowing him to keep his belongings for as long as he wanted was not a big deal. Communication beforehand may have helped.

As you transition into different roles, be gentle with yourself and your loved one. Everyone is doing the best they can.

Scripture

"Sing to God, sing in praise of his name, extol him who rides on the clouds[a]; rejoice before him—his name is the Lord. A father to the fatherless, a defender of widows, I s God in his holy dwelling" (Psalm 68:4-5 NIV).

Prayer

Father, we come before You this day. Our heart is heavy with difficult decisions surrounding the care and safety of our loved ones. Lead and guide us as we assume more control over responsibilities once assumed with ease and capability by our aging parent. Give us grace as we communicate and execute what must be done. Allow our parents to understand the need for change. Give us strength and compassion throughout this difficult season. Amen.

Helpful Resources

Tuesdays with Morrie by Mitch Albom available on Amazon: https://amzn.to/2UX4H0h

Anticipatory Grief

Anticipatory grief is an ever-present emotion of the soul and spirit. A festering wound, anticipatory grief may first surface with the initial sign of illness, a new diagnosis of cancer, physical or mental decline.

Caregiving comes with prepackaged grief waiting to jump out like a Jack-in the-Box toy at the most inopportune moments. The pain may resurface as your loved one complains of new symptoms. Perhaps Alzheimer's Disease is creating a slow, endless decline. Or maybe your once strong spouse morphs into a weak unrecognizable partner.

Anticipatory Grief

Caregiver grief is characterized by anticipatory grief. Anticipatory grief is defined as the loss felt before a loved one dies. The pain felt is just as hurtful as grief following death. Grief rips at the heart.

Anticipatory grief comes when changes in your loved one are manifested perhaps through dementia. The person you once knew is gone.

Loss of control over mounting symptoms leaves us with a sense of loss. Perhaps an accident has left your loved one handicapped and helpless. Mentally, we grapple to come to terms with the new norm. We are helpless as the disease process possesses our loved one.

Caregivers may feel grief on a daily basis. Their feelings may be more pronounced than those who are not directly participating in the demands of caregiving. Do not compare yourself to others.

My own caregiving journey was overshadowed by anticipatory grief. The following paragraph is an excerpt from my book, *Before You Depart: God's Touch Before Eternity*.

At the age of 90, my dad's diagnosis with cancer of the esophagus threatened my existing reality. The journey ahead lurked with phantasmal shadows on all sides. My head was filled with magnified fear, dread and apprehension. Denial whispered that my dad was not elderly and the prayerful plea...*I'm not ready for my dad to die.*

Honor your grief. Share with someone that loves you. The feelings are real. Cry when needed. Pray to God who always hears your cry.

Scripture

*"Even though I walk through the sunless valley of the shadow of death,
I fear no evil, for You are with me;
Your rod [to protect] and Your staff [to guide], they comfort and console me."* (Psalm 23:4 AMP).

*The cords of death surrounded me,
And the streams of ungodliness and torrents of destruction terrified me.
The cords of Sheol (the nether world, the place of the dead) surrounded me;
The snares of death confronted me.
In my distress [when I seemed surrounded] I called upon the Lord
And cried to my God for help;
He heard my voice from His temple,
And my cry for help came before Him, into His very ears.* (Psalm 18:4-6 AMP).

Prayer

Father, you know those whose hearts are burdened with grief and endless responsibility. Help them in this time of need and bring comfort to their heavy hearts. You are acquainted with their grief. Give them a special strength for their journey today. Amen.

Grief for the Caregiver

The heartbreak of grief touches all individuals. Grief differs for all of us.

My grief experience following my dad's death fueled further research, culminating in my Caregiver Series and my capstone project while working on my masters degree. This chapter is the focus of information gleaned from my research of Prolonged Grief Disorder in caregivers.

Research indicates that most people are nearing the end of their grief journey in approximately six months following the death of a loved one. Grief may not be completely over, however sadness and ruminating about the loved one begin to subside. Acute grief is described as a common experience.

Prolonged Grief Disorder, or complicated grief is displayed in several different circumstances surrounding the loss of someone or something significant, including the death of a child, spouse or a traumatic life experience. Research has indicated that approximately 20% of individuals who are bereaved will experience Prolonged Grief Disorder.

Grieving caregivers experience unique stressors during the course of their caregiving journey. These stressors contribute to prolonged grief. Physical strain, social, emotion stressors and financial hardship during caregiving lead to an increase in mortality and other physical stress and disease. The state of bereavement also carries with it the risk factor for impaired immunity and poorer overall physical health.

Prolonged Grief Disorder is characterized by an increased risk of suicide, loneliness, substance abuse, physical and emotional disability, gastrointestinal issues, sleep disturbance and even death. Symptoms of decline are experienced by older caregivers. Younger female caregivers and those with lower socioeconomic status experience greater emotional stress.

Other physical complications include cancer, high blood pressure, heart disease and increased risk of hospitalization. Individuals suffering from mental disorders such as bipolar disorder and depression have exacerbations. Increased symptoms of anxiety, or panic attacks may occur.

Contributing Factors to Prolonged Grief Disorder.

Sometimes a loved one's symptoms are difficult to witness and control. Pain, shortness of breath, vomiting, fatigue, general decline, and fear of death contribute to Prolonged Grief Disorder. Perception of care for the loved one as being poor, family conflict and strife at the end-of -life affects the caregiver.

Isolation during the caregiving process, difficulty finding adequate support and overcoming caregiver exhaustion contribute to bereavement difficulty. Other contributing factors include previous symptoms of depression, a lower socioeconomic status, and a younger age of the caregiver. The inability of the caregiver to forgive also complicates grief.

Caregivers whose loved one has cancer and dementia experience greater physical and psychological burdens than caregivers of diabetes or those caring for frail elderly individuals.

The Grieving Process

Dr. Kubler-Ross formulated a grief theory consisting of five stages: denial, anger, bargaining, depression and acceptance. The stages of grief come and go and often overlap. Stages do not occur in sequence; however most bereaved individuals experience each stage at one time or another during their grief journey. The theory gives structure and meaning to the confusing state of grief and hope for eventual healing.

The first stage, denial, is characterized by the disbelief that the loved one is gone. The death cannot be true.

The second stage of anger includes a variety of emotions. People may blame and direct anger at doctors, self, the deceased, others in the environment and possibly God. Dr Kubler-Ross theorized that anger was a necessary part of the healing process. Other emotions included sadness, panic, hurt, loneliness and emotional pain.

Anger was found to be difficult to express toward the deceased. Kubler-Ross believed that the bereaved must be allowed to express anger concerning the deceased or God in nonjudgmental ways.

The third stage is bargaining. An example of bargaining would be asking God to intervene before and after the death. Asking

God to return life to what was previous before the illness or death occurred. Remaining in the past is a way of bargaining to relieve the pain of grief.

Depression is the fourth stage in response to the death of a loved one. Grief from depressions has various degrees of pain and sadness at different times. Depression during grief is necessary and vital to the healing process.

Acceptance, the final stage is the realization that the loved one is physically gone and the loss is permanent. Acceptance include the reintegration of life without the deceased.

Triggers for Grief

Common triggers for grief feelings include the deceased loved one's birthday, the anniversary of their death and the Christmas season. During these times the feelings of loss and pain often return.

On my dad's birthday after he died, we had a party complete with his favorite cake. Later anniversary dates weren't as difficult. My approach was to celebrate and remember the good times we had.

Grief is messy, painful, difficult work. Putting a time limit on grief is challenging. Each person is unique in their approach to the loss of a loved one. Grieving in American society can be problematic because feelings of depression are not easily accepted. Friends may not be able to relate to your feelings of loss.

You may suffer from Prolonged Grief Disorder as I did after the death of my dad. I was a young caregiver, and my dad was one of my last living relatives. Grief consumed me for a time and I became very depressed. The Hospice that provided Dad's end-of-life care provided a grief counselor. I continued counseling for several years following his death.

During this difficult time, find support. Grief counselors can offer nonjudgmental assistance during your journey of loss. Not everyone knows how you are feeling. A counselor can provide a listening ear to express your emotions of loss, anger, guilt, and despair.

Honor your feelings of sadness and memories that bring tears. Honor your loved one's life and the memories that will always live in your heart. Allow yourself time to heal, yet try to avoid continual despair. These feelings can overwhelm and debilitate us. One person taught me that I could visit those feelings, but I did not have to live there.

Help is available. Reach out. Grief support groups are held in some churches and funeral homes. If your loved one is on Hospice a support group following death is usually provided.

If you have feelings of continued grief and depression, consider seeing your physician. Over time, the chemicals in our brains can become unbalanced. Antidepressants can help.

Stay in touch with your primary care physician while you are busy with caregiving and when your role had ended. If you do not have a primary care provider, get one. Caregivers tend to neglect their own physical health.

Your loved one would want you to live life to the fullest. Be sure to take good care of yourself during the grief process just as you did while you were caregiving.

God bless you now and always.

Scripture

"And the Lord will continually guide you, and satisfy your soul in scorched and dry places, and give strength to your bones; and you will be like a watered garden, and like a spring of water whose waters do not fail" (Isaiah 58:11 AMP).

Prayer

Father, provide comfort to each caregiver as they journey through the difficult, heartbreaking emotions of grief. Strengthen weakened hearts. Give each one the support needed. Provide in their time of need and loss. You are acquainted with everything that confronts us. Manifest your love and peace during this difficult season. Provide health, healing and wholeness in Your perfect time. Amen.

Resources

Google "Grief Support Groups in my area."

Google "Certified grief counselor near me."

One Day at a Time

One day at a time is an essential way to approach caregiving. Looking ahead into the vast unknown of chronic illness and pending death compounds worries and fears. Hope is dashed. Our worst imaginations blossom into dread.

God never intended us to live in the future. Only He knows what will be. All we have is now. Today.

Today is enough.

God's grace for this day is sufficient. God is present with you, your family and your loved one. Pray for this day and what you are needing now. Maybe you need extra patience or strength.

Pray for tomorrow. Hold on to hope for answered prayer. Then let your prayers and tomorrow rest at the foot of the cross.

Sometimes when my world is turned upside down and I don't know where to begin, I wake up and repeat out loud, "This is the day the Lord has made, rejoice and be glad in it." This short praise to God reminds me that He is with me. He is in control. He is taking care of me today.

My heart is lifted and worries fall away. God alone can usher me through whatever muddy swamp lies ahead. Just for today.

Waking up and praising God for the day awakens the mind and spirit to the good that surrounds us. Maybe the beautiful sunrise, the smile on your loved one's face, or just another day to enjoy the one you are caring for.

There is beauty and good all around us. Take time to enjoy those gifts even in the midst of your crisis.

God is with you today and every day. Rest in His loving presence.

Scripture

"So do not worry about tomorrow; for tomorrow will worry about itself. Each day has enough trouble of its own" (Matthew 6:34 AMP).

Prayer

Father,

Be with each caregiver today. Give them all their needs for this day alone. Help them to cast all their cares onto You. Give them the assurance You are with them. Let them know in their hearts that You will never, never leave them nor forsake them. Today and every day. Amen.

About the Author

Nanette M. Holloway, MS, RN was a caregiver to both her mother and father. Both died from cancer. Her difficult journey through the muddy swamp of caregiving led her to write this publication. Her hope is that you will benefit from her experience.

Holloway is a registered nurse currently working in home health. Prior career choices included working as a Hospice RN, caring for individuals and their families with chronic illnesses and end-of-life issues. She approaches nursing as a ministry, caring for the body, mind and spirit.

Nanette and her husband live in the Midwest on eighty acres. They have two grown sons whom she homeschooled.

Gardening is a favorite past time. She and her family cultivated a vineyard and large vegetable garden, taking their produce to the local farmer's market. She also raises flowers and has completed the Master Gardener course through Oklahoma State University.

Nanette holds a Master's Degree in Nursing Education. While obtaining her Master's she rediscovered her love of writing.

You can follow her on Facebook and Linked In. Subscribe to her blog at: nanetteholloway.com. Connect with God in the beauty of the garden and follow her caregiving blogs.

Be sure to post a review of *Coping Skills for Caregivers* on Amazon and Goodreads. That is, if you get some downtime during your caregiving duties.

Other Books by
Nanette M. Holloway, MS, RN

Gratitude Journal for Caregivers

Coping Skills for Caregivers Workbook

Before You Depart: God's Touch Before Eternity